"Way to God"

A Scholarly Guide to Islamic Beliefs, Practices, and Spiritual Journey

Sahibzada

Copyright © *Sahibzada*, 2025
All Rights Reserved

This book is subject to the condition that no part of this book is to be reproduced, transmitted in any form or means; electronic or mechanical, stored in a retrieval system, photocopied, recorded, scanned, or otherwise. Any of these actions require the proper written permission of the author.

Table of Contents

Acknowledgement 4

About the Author 5

Chapter 1 Tawhid and Divine Love 6

Chapter 2: Love for the Prophet Muhammad ﷺ – The Essence of Faith and the Path to Divine Closeness 11

Chapter 3: Duties of the Companions of the Prophet ﷺ and the Household of the Prophet ﷺ in Light of the Qur'an and Hadith 16

Chapter 4: The Four Major Schools of Thought in Islam 21

Chapter 5: The Recitation of the Holy Qur'an – Importance of Learning Arabic and Understanding Its Meaning 31

Chapter 6: Bay'ah – A Sacred Covenant in Islam 37

Chapter 7: Bid'ah (Innovation) in the Light of Qur'an and Hadith 43

Chapter 8: Jannah (Paradise) – The Ultimate Reward for Believers 48

Chapter 9: Jihad – The True 59

Concept of Struggle in Islam 59

Chapter 10: The Remembrance of Allah (Dhikr) – The Path to Spiritual Elevation 65

Chapter 11: Reciting Darood-e-Pak – A Dhikr That Pleases Both Allah SWT and the Prophet ﷺ 71

Conclusion: The Way to God – A Journey of Knowledge, Love, and Spiritual Transformation 76

Acknowledgement

Undoubtedly, there are some personalities who are like radiant light; they do not merely come into this world to live but to ignite the lamps of guidance, illuminate paths, and fill hearts with love, wisdom, and sincerity.

Among such blessed souls were my beloved father, **Sahibzada Ghulam Siddique Ahmed Naqshbandi Mujaddidi (May Allah have mercy on him)**—my world, my identity, and the very reason for my existence. Whatever I am today, whatever I have learned, understood, or reflected upon in life, is a direct reflection of his teachings, his love, and his exemplary character.

He did not just influence me through words but through his actions, his prayers, and his spiritual presence—each of which continues to illuminate my path. His every command was advice, his every smile was a prayer, and his every action was a profound lesson in itself.

He was not just a father to me but also a guide, a teacher, and a beacon of spiritual light. He remains so ever present in my heart, in my thoughts, and in my prayers.

May Allah ﷻ fill his grave with eternal light, elevate his rank in the Hereafter, and grant us all the ability to live by the values and teachings he embodied.

About the Author

Sahibzada Shahid Siddiq, is a distinguished Islamic thinker, spiritual guide, and community leader currently residing in England. He is the **Founder and President of Anjuman**

Gulzar-e-Madinah International, an organization devoted to spreading the love of the Prophet Muhammad ﷺ, nurturing spiritual development, and promoting Islamic knowledge across the globe.

He holds an **MBA from London, England**, and has successfully established himself in the business sector while remaining deeply committed to his religious and spiritual responsibilities. Balancing his professional career and spiritual mission, he continues to inspire individuals toward a life of devotion, sincerity, and service to humanity.

Sahibzada Shahid Siddiq inherits a rich spiritual legacy as the **Khalifa (spiritual successor) of Gulzar-e-Madinah, Gujrat Shareef**, and is a devoted disciple of **Iftikhar-ul-Mushaikh Hazrat Ghulam Siddique Ahmad Naqshbandi Mujaddidi** (رحمة الله) His teacher's guidance has been a cornerstone in shaping his path, knowledge, and spiritual insight.

A lifelong seeker of truth, a lover of the Prophet ﷺ, and a carrier of the illuminating torch of his guide's teachings, he continues to serve the Ummah, through his writings, lectures, and spiritual mentorship, striving to connect hearts with Allah ﷻ and His Beloved Prophet Muhammad ﷺ.

Chapter 1:

Tawhid and Divine Love

Introduction to Tawhid – The Foundation of Islam

Tawhid (توحيد), the concept of the Oneness of God, is the very foundation and central pillar of Islam. It is the first article of faith and the bedrock upon which all Islamic beliefs and practices are established. The term **Tawhid** linguistically stems from the Arabic root **"wahhada"**, meaning **"to unify" or "to declare as one."** In Islamic theology, Tawhid refers to affirming the **absolute oneness, uniqueness, and incomparability of Allah (God)** in His Essence, Attributes, and Actions.

Allah ﷻ is not only One in being but also free from all forms of plurality, partners, resemblance, or similitude. He is self-sufficient and independent of all creation, while everything in existence depends upon Him.

The importance of Tawhid is evident in the **first part of the Shahadah (Declaration of Faith):**

> "La ilaha illa Allah"
> (There is no god but Allah).

This concise statement encapsulates the rejection of all false deities and the affirmation that Allah alone is the One worthy of worship.

1.2 Categories of Tawhid

Islamic scholars have explained Tawhid in three primary categories to deepen understanding and avoid confusion. These are:

1. Taw heed al-Rububiyyah (Oneness in Lordship)

This aspect affirms that **Allah alone is the Creator, Sustainer, Owner, and Controller of everything in the universe.** No being shares His power or authority in creation or sustenance.

> *"Say, 'Who provides for you from the sky and the earth? Or who owns hearing and sight? And who brings the living out of the dead and brings the dead out of the living? And who arranges [every] matter?' They will say, 'Allah.' So say, 'Then will you not fear Him?'"*
> **(Surah Yunus 10:31)**

2. Tawhid al-Uluhiyyah (Oneness in Worship)

This refers to **singling out Allah alone for all forms of worship**, including prayer, fasting, charity, supplication, reliance, and love. None other than Allah is to be worshipped, and all acts of devotion must be directed solely to Him.

> *"And your God is One God. There is no deity [worthy of worship] except Him, the Entirely Merciful, the Especially Merciful."*
> **(Surah Al-Baqarah 2:163)**

3. Tawhid al-Asma wa al-Sifat (Oneness in Names and Attributes)

This aspect affirms that **Allah possesses the most beautiful names and perfect attributes**, as mentioned in the Qur'an and authentic Hadith, without resembling His creation or likening Him to anything.

> *"There is nothing like unto Him, and He is the All-Hearing, the All-Seeing."*
> **(Surah Ash-Shura 42:11)**

1.3. The Relationship Between Tawhid and Divine Love

While Tawhid is often taught as a theological construct, it is incomplete without **deep spiritual love (maḥabbah)** for the One True God. Tawhid is not merely intellectual acknowledgement but a **heartfelt connection** with the Divine. The essence of belief is not just to know that Allah is One but to **love Him, revere Him, seek closeness to Him, and submit joyfully to His Will.**

In truth, **Tawhid without Divine Love becomes dry theology**, while love without Tawhid becomes misguided emotion. The **perfect harmony of Tawhid and Divine Love** is what brings balance to a Muslim's life—both in belief and practice.

> *"But those who believe are stronger in love for Allah."* **(Surah Al-Baqarah 2:165)**

This verse signifies that the highest quality of believers is not just monotheism but **deep, sincere love for Allah**. Such love surpasses any worldly affection and becomes the engine of one's obedience, sincerity, and spiritual yearning.

1.4. Manifestation of Divine Love Through Worship and Obedience

The true test of love for Allah is **obedience to His commands and emulation of His Messenger** ﷺ. Worship in Islam is not a ritual devoid of emotion but an expression of love, reverence, and submission. A believer who understands Tawhid and loves Allah naturally finds delight in prayer, fasting, charity, remembrance (Dhikr), and following the Sunnah.

> *"Say [O Prophet], 'If you love Allah, then follow me; Allah will love you and forgive your sins.'"* **(Surah Al-Imran 3:31)**

Thus, love for Allah necessitates love for the Prophet Muhammad ﷺ and obedience to his teachings. This creates a beautiful chain of love: **from the heart of a believer to the Prophet ﷺ, and from the Prophet ﷺ to Allah.**

1.5. How Tawhid Shapes the MuslimIdentity

A Muslim who fully understands Tawhid and internalizes Divine Love:

- **Finds purpose in life**: Knowing that Allah created them for His worship.
- **Remains firm in trials**: Relying on Allah's mercy and wisdom.
- **Seeks Divine Pleasure**: Prioritizing obedience over worldly gain.
- **Fights inner desires (Jihad al-Nafs)**: Recognizing that Allah's love is greater than worldly temptations.
- **Lives with sincerity (Ikhlas)**: Performing every deed only for Allah's acceptance.

1.6. The Spiritual Dimensions of Tawhid

Sufis and scholars of inner purification (tazkiyah) emphasize the **internal realization of Tawhid,** beyond verbal declaration. They teach that real Tawhid means **detaching the heart from all other than Allah,** relying solely on Him, loving only for His sake, and fearing none but Him.

Such spiritual Tawhid leads to **contentment (qanā'ah), trust (tawakkul), sincerity (ikhlāṣ),** and **humility (tawāḍu')**—the hallmarks of a God-conscious life.

1.7. Conclusion: Tawhid – The First Step on the Way to God

In conclusion, **Tawhid is not merely a belief but the gateway to the spiritual journey toward Allah.** It is the soul of worship, the source of love, and the path to eternal success. Without Tawhid, faith is meaningless, and without Divine Love, belief becomes hollow.

The one who internalizes Tawhid with love becomes a true servant ('abd) of Allah, walking the way to God with sincerity, devotion, and tranquillity. Tawhid, thus, is not just theology—it is **life itself.**

Chapter 2:

Love for the Prophet Muhammad ﷺ – The Essence of Faith and the Path to Divine Closeness

2.1. Introduction: The Centrality of Prophetic Love in Islam

In the grand edifice of Islam, after belief in the Oneness of Allah (Tawhid), the most sacred and essential element is **love for the Prophet Muhammad ﷺ**. This love is not a supplementary sentiment—it is the **very core of faith (Iman)** and a vital condition of spiritual elevation. Allah has made the love and obedience of His beloved Prophet ﷺ a **criterion of faith** and a **pathway to Divine Pleasure**.

> *"Say [O Prophet], 'If you love Allah, then follow me; Allah will love you and forgive your sins.'"* **(Surah Aal-Imran 3:31)**

Thus, love for the Prophet ﷺ is not merely a matter of affection but an **obligatory component of belief**, deeply rooted in the Qur'an and Hadith, reflected in the lives of the Companions, and upheld through centuries of Islamic tradition.

2.2 The Prophet ﷺ as the Mercy to All CreationAllah describes the Prophet ﷺ in the Qur'an as:

> *"And We have not sent you [O Prophet] except as a mercy to the worlds."*
> **(Surah Al-Anbiya 21:107)**

This ayah establishes that the Prophet Muhammad ﷺ is not only a spiritual guide for Muslims but a **universal source of mercy** for all creation—humans, animals, jinn, and even the environment. His teachings are the light that dispelled the darkness of ignorance, injustice, and oppression.

To love him is to love **mercy, guidance, compassion, knowledge, and righteousness**, all of which he embodied.

2.3 The Prophet's ﷺ Role in Divine Revelation and Guidance

The Prophet ﷺ is not merely a conveyor of Divine Message—he is the **interpreter, the living embodiment, and the perfect example of that message**. His character is described in the Qur'an as:

> *"Indeed, you are of an exalted character."*
> **(Surah Al-Qalam 68:4)**

He explained, practiced, and demonstrated the Qur'an in action. As his wife Sayyidah A'ishah ؓ said:

> *"His character was the Qur'an."*
> **(Sahih Muslim)**

Therefore, love for the Prophet ﷺ is essentially love for the Qur'an and love for Islam in its complete form.

2.4 The Obligation to Love the Prophet ﷺ More Than All Else

The Prophet ﷺ explicitly stated:

> *"None of you will have faith until he loves me more than his father, his children, and all of mankind."*
> **(Sahih al-Bukhari)**

This Hadith firmly establishes that **true faith is incomplete without surpassing love for the Prophet** ﷺ. This love must exceed all worldly loves—family, wealth, desires, and even one's own self.

This is not fanaticism but spiritual realism. The Prophet ﷺ brought us guidance, rescued us from darkness, and opened the path to eternal salvation. How can any love be greater than love for such a benefactor?

2.5 Manifestations of Love for the Prophet ﷺ

True love for the Prophet ﷺ is not limited to mere verbal praise or poetic expression. It must be **manifested in practice and conduct**, including:

- **Following his Sunnah (traditions)**
- **Defending his honor**
- **Sending abundant Salawat (blessings)upon him**
- **Learning his Sirah (life) and embodying his character**
- **Respecting his family (Ahl al-Bayt), companions (Sahaba), and teachings**
- **Celebrating his remembrance and teachings with reverence and gratitude**

> *"Indeed, Allah and His angels send blessings upon the Prophet. O you who have believed, send blessings upon him and peace in abundance."*
> **(Surah Al-Ahzab 33:56)**

2.6 The Path to Divine Closeness Through Prophetic Love

Prophetic love is not merely emotional—it is transformative. It reshapes a person's inner self, inclines the heart toward righteousness, and elevates one's station in the sight of Allah. The more one increases in love for the Prophet ﷺ, the more one becomes beloved by Allah.

> *"Whoever obeys the Messenger has indeed obeyed Allah."*
> **(Surah An-Nisa 4:80)**

This divine equation indicates that **obedience to the Prophet ﷺ is equivalent to obedience to Allah**, and love for him is love for Allah's commands.

The Companions (Sahaba), the greatest generation of believers, demonstrated this love practically—abandoning their homes, sacrificing their lives, and following every word of the Prophet ﷺ. Their love was not ritualistic—it was passionate, complete, and unconditional.

2.7 Historical Expressions of Love for the Prophet ﷺ

Throughout history, scholars, saints, poets, and rulers expressed immense love for the Prophet ﷺ:

- **Imam Al-Busiri's Qasida al-Burda** remains a classic ode of praise and love.
- **Imam Abu Hanifa, Imam Malik,** and others would show deep reverence whenmentioning the Prophet's ﷺ name.
- **Great Sufi saints,** like **Hazrat Abdul Qadir Jilani** (رحمة الله). emphasized love and attachment to the Prophet ﷺ as a central element of the spiritual path (Tariqah).

This love continues today in the hearts of believers who honour Mawlid (Prophet's birth), practice his Sunnah, and express their yearning in Duas and poetry.

2.8 Love for the Prophet's ﷺ Family and Companions

Love for the Prophet ﷺ is incomplete without love and respect for his **Ahl al-Bayt (Household)** and his **Sahaba (Companions)**. They were chosen by Allah to be his closest supporters and transmitters of his teachings.

> *"Say: I do not ask you any reward for it except love for my near relatives."*
> **(Surah Ash-Shura 42:23)**

The Prophet ﷺ emphasized loving his family and treating his companions with reverence. Any disrespect towards them is a **betrayal of prophetic love** and an insult to those who preserved our religion.

2.9 Conclusion: Love for the Prophet ﷺ – The Light That Illuminates the Path to Allah

To love the Prophet Muhammad ﷺ is to live in his light, walk in his path, and seek closeness to the One who sent him. He is the **gateway to Divine Love**, the **embodiment of mercy**, and the **eternal guide for all hearts seeking truth**.

The heart that holds love for him never goes astray. It finds tranquillity in his remembrance, strength in his teachings, and elevation in his footsteps.

> *"And know that the Messenger of Allah is among you."*
> **(Surah Al-Hujurat 49:7)**

Indeed, for the believer, the Prophet ﷺ is not a figure of the past—**he is ever-present in our faith, our hearts, and our path to Allah.**

Chapter 3:

Duties of the Companions of the Prophet ﷺ and the Household of the Prophet ﷺ in Light of the Qur'an and Hadith

3.1 Introduction: The Torchbearers of Prophetic Light

The Prophet Muhammad ﷺ was divinely chosen as the Seal of Prophethood, the final guide to humanity. However, Allah, in His wisdom, appointed a special group to accompany him during his earthly mission—**the Companions (Sahaba)** and **the members of his purified Household (Ahl al-Bayt)**. Their role was not passive; they were the **first recipients, preservers, interpreters,** and **transmitters** of the prophetic legacy.

This chapter explores their **duties, virtues**, and **the divine responsibility placed upon them**, all in the light of the **Qur'an, Hadith**, and **Islamic tradition**. Understanding their roles is essential to appreciating the continuity and integrity of Islam.

3.2 Definition and Significance of the Companions (Sahaba)

A **Sahabi (Companion)** is defined in classical Islamic scholarship as:

> "A person who met the Prophet ﷺ while believing in him and died upon Islam."

This definition includes men, women, young, old, free, and enslaved individuals who lived during the time of the Prophet ﷺ and were part of his mission. They represent the **first generation of Muslims**, and Allah praises them in multiple places in the Qur'an:

> *"And the first forerunners [in the faith] among the Muhajirun and the Ansar and those who followed them with good conduct—Allah is pleased with them and they are pleased with Him."* **(Surah At-Tawbah 9:100)**

Their significance lies not merely in chronological proximity but in their unwavering **sacrifice, love, obedience,** and **transmission of the deen (religion).**

3.3 The Duties and Contributions of the Sahaba

3.3.1 Preservation of the Qur'an

The Sahaba had the sacred duty of **receiving, memorizing, writing, and preserving the Qur'an** as it was revealed. Notably:

- **Zayd ibn Thabit** ﷺ served as a scribe and later compiled the Qur'an during Abu Bakr's ﷺ Caliphate.

- **Hundreds of Sahaba memorized the Qur'an**, ensuring its preservation through both oral and written traditions.

3.3.2 Transmission of Hadith

Hadith literature—the sayings, actions, and approvals of the Prophet ﷺ—has reached us entirely through the Sahaba. Notable transmitters include:

- **Abu Hurairah** ﷺ – narrated over 5,000 Hadith.

- **A'ishah** ﷺ – the Mother of the Believers and one of the foremost scholars.

- **Abdullah ibn Umar, Abdullah ibn Abbas, Anas ibn Malik, Jabir ibn Abdullah,** and others played foundational roles.

3.3.3 Spreading the Message Globally

After the Prophet's ﷺ demise, the Sahaba spread Islam far and wide:

- **In Arabia:** through regional da'wah and administrative leadership.
- **In Persia, Rome, Africa, India:** through military expeditions and peaceful preaching. Their travels were not colonial conquests but **divine missions to convey Islam**, often involving intense sacrifice.

3.3.4 Establishment of Islamic Governance

The **Rightly Guided Caliphs (Khulafa-e-Rashideen)**—Abu Bakr, Umar, Uthman, and Ali ؓ —implemented **Islamic justice, shura (consultation), social welfare, and public administration** as practical extensions of Prophetic Sunnah.

3.3.5 Moral Role Modeling and Spiritual Transmission

The Sahaba were the first role models for Muslims. Their humility, worship, simplicity, sacrifice, and love for the Prophet ﷺ serve as living examples of Islamic values. Their interactions with the Prophet ﷺ became a blueprint for Muslim behaviour in every generation.

3.4 The Elevated Station of Ahl al-Bayt (Household of the Prophet ﷺ)

The **Ahl al-Bayt** includes the Prophet's ﷺ closest family:

- **Sayyidah Fatimah** ؓ
- **Imam Hasan and Imam Husayn** ؓ
- **Sayyiduna Ali ibn Abi Talib** ؓ

- And other noble family members from the descendants of the Prophet ﷺ.

The Qur'an explicitly honours them:

> *"Indeed, Allah desires to remove impurity from you, O People of the House, and to purify you completely."* **(Surah Al-Ahzab 33:33)**

Their station is not only due to lineage but due to their **faith, piety, sacrifice**, and **closeness to the Prophet ﷺ in belief and action**.

3.5 Duties and Contributions of the Ahl al-Bayt

3.5.1 Upholding Spiritual Leadership

After the Prophet ﷺ, many members of Ahl al-Bayt became **spiritual leaders, scholars, and reformers**, such as:

- **Imam Zayn al-Abidin**
- **Imam Muhammad al-Baqir**
- **Imam Ja'far al-Sadiq**

Their knowledge was foundational for many Islamic sciences, including Fiqh, Hadith, and Tasawwuf.

3.5.2 The Martyrdom of Imam Husayn ؓ

The sacrifice at **Karbala** is a pivotal moment in Islamic history. Imam Husayn ؓ, the beloved grandson of the Prophet ﷺ, stood against tyranny and injustice, choosing martyrdom over compromise. His blood became a symbol of **truth over falsehood**, and his sacrifice remains a **universal lesson of standing for divine values**.

3.5.3 Preserving Prophetic Ethics and Morality

The Ahl al-Bayt, being closest in blood to the Prophet ﷺ, carried his manners, compassion, and integrity in the most intimate form. Their actions reflected the Prophetic legacy in the most pristine form and continue to inspire Muslims in every age.

3.6 The Unified Respect for Sahaba and Ahl al-Bayt

It is a **sacred duty for every Muslim** to **love and honour both the Sahaba and Ahl al-Bayt** without creating conflict between them. The Prophet ﷺ said:

> *"Fear Allah regarding my companions. Do not make them the target [of criticism] after me. Whoever loves them, loves them because of his love for me. Whoever hates them, hates them because of his hatred for me."* **(Tirmidhi)**

Both groups served the Prophet ﷺ and preserved the religion. Dishonor towards either is a sign of deviation and ingratitude.

3.7 Conclusion: The Companions and Ahl al-Bayt – Pillars of the Ummah

The **Sahaba and Ahl al-Bayt are the pillars upon which the structure of Islam rests** after the Prophet ﷺ. Their loyalty, wisdom, and service to the Deen preserved the message of Islam in both spirit and structure. For students of knowledge, scholars, and believers alike, **love, respect, and emulation of these noble souls is part of the path to Divine Closeness**.

They are not merely historical figures—they are **spiritual guides**, **intellectual architects**, and **luminous stars of guidance** for every age.

> *"My companions are like stars; whoever among them you follow, you will be rightly guided."* **(Musnad Ahmad)**

Chapter 4:

The Four Major Schools of Thought in Islam

4.1 Introduction: The Framework of Islamic Jurisprudence (Fiqh)

Islam is a comprehensive way of life, addressing every aspect of human existence—spiritual, moral, social, economic, and legal. While the Qur'an and Sunnah form the primary sources of Islamic law (Shari'ah), the practical application of these principles in the diverse contexts of life requires a systematic methodology. This gave rise to **Islamic Jurisprudence (Fiqh)**—the science of understanding and deriving legal rulings from the sources of Islam.

To ensure consistency, clarity, and legal rigour, early scholars developed organized schools of thought (**Madhāhib**, plural of **Madhhab**), each grounded in the Qur'an and Sunnah but differing slightly in methodology and legal reasoning. The development of these schools was not a division but rather **a manifestation of intellectual richness** within the unity of Islam.

4.2 What Is a Madhhab?

A **Madhhab** is a structured school of jurisprudential thought developed by a qualified **Mujtahid Imam**, who was deeply grounded in the Qur'an, Hadith, consensus (Ijma'), and analogical reasoning (Qiyas). A Madhhab provides:

- A **systematic methodology** to derive rulings from sources.
- A **codified legal framework** for the practical application of Shari'ah.

- A **scholarly tradition** for preserving and transmitting Islamic knowledge.

The existence of multiple Madhāhib is **not a contradiction to unity** but rather a **natural result of scholarly ijtihad (independent reasoning)** and the vastness of Islamic sources.

4.3 Why Are There Four Major Madhāhib?

During the early centuries of Islam, many scholars developed jurisprudential methodologies. However, four schools reached such a level of scholarly depth, precision, and widespread acceptance that they became the dominant Madhāhib of Sunni Islam. These are:

1. Hanafi Madhhab
2. Maliki Madhhab
3. Shafi'i Madhhab
4. Hanbali Madhhab

Their widespread institutional teaching, meticulous documentation, and scholarly acceptance preserved them across the Muslim world.

4.4 The Hanafi Madhhab

4.4.1 Founder: Imam Abu Hanifah (699–767 CE)

- Born in **Kufa (Iraq)**, Imam Abu Hanifah (Nu'man ibn Thabit) was known for his intelligence, integrity, and deep reasoning.
- He met many **Tabi'een (Successors of the Sahaba)** and was deeply influenced by them.

4.4.2 Methodology

- Strong reliance on the **Qur'an and Hadith** as primary sources.

- Emphasis on **Qiyas (analogy)** and **Istihsan (juridical preference)** to apply rulings in new situations.
- Consideration of **public interest (Maslahah)** and **local customs ('Urf)** when deriving laws.

4.4.3 Contributions

- The **first structured legal school** in Islam.
- Legal reasoning used to answer **new situations not explicitly mentioned in the Qur'an and Hadith.**
- Thousands of legal issues discussed and documented.

4.4.4 Spread

- Widely followed in **Turkey, Central Asia, Indian Subcontinent, Balkans, Egypt, Syria, Iraq**, and other regions.
- The most widely practiced Madhhab among Muslims today.

4.5 The Maliki Madhhab

4.5.1 Founder: Imam Malik ibn Anas (711–795 CE)

- Born and lived in **Madinah**, the city of the Prophet ﷺ.
- Studied under the **students of the Sahaba** and was a master of Hadith and Fiqh.

4.5.2 Methodology

- Gave great weight to the **'Amal (practice) of the people of Madinah**, considering it a reflection of the Sunnah.
- Emphasis on **Hadith, Ijma'**, and **Maslahah Mursalah (public welfare)**.

- Moderate use of analogy and preference.

4.5.3 Contributions

- Author of **"Al-Muwatta"**, one of the earliest Hadith and Fiqh compilations.
- Preserved **Prophetic practices** and early Islamic legal thought.

4.5.4 Spread

- Predominantly followed in **North and West Africa, Sudan, parts of the Arabian Peninsula**, and **some areas of the Gulf**.

4.6 The Shafi'i Madhhab

4.6.1 Founder: Imam Muhammad ibn Idris al-Shafi'i (767–820 CE)

- Born in **Gaza, Palestine**, and raised in **Makkah**.
- A student of **Imam Malik** and a teacher to **Imam Ahmad ibn Hanbal**.

4.6.2 Methodology

- Known for **systematizing the science of Usul al-Fiqh (Principles of Jurisprudence)**.
- Strong emphasis on the **Qur'an, Hadith**, then **Ijma'** and **Qiyas**.
- Developed a **balanced methodology** between Hadith and rational derivation.

4.6.3 Contributions

- Author of **"Al-Risalah"**, a foundational text in Usul al-Fiqh.

- Laid the groundwork for how legal reasoning should be done in an Islamic framework.

4.6.4 Spread

- Followed in **East Africa (Somalia, Kenya), Southeast Asia (Indonesia, Malaysia), Egypt, parts of Yemen**, and **South India**.

4.7 The Hanbali Madhhab

4.7.1 Founder: Imam Ahmad ibn Hanbal (780–855 CE)

- Born in **Baghdad**, a student of **Imam Shafi'i**.
- Revered for his **deep knowledge of Hadith and steadfastness in trials**.

4.7.2 Methodology

- Strict adherence to **Qur'an and authentic Hadith**.
- Limited reliance on Qiyas, only when absolutely necessary.
- Avoided using personal reasoning when a text was available.

4.7.3 Contributions

- Compiled the monumental Hadith collection **"Musnad Ahmad ibn Hanbal"**.
- Preserved the traditionalist approach during times of doctrinal debates.

4.7.4 Spread

- Followed in **Saudi Arabia, Qatar**, and parts of **the Gulf region**.

4.8 Unity in Diversity: The Harmony of the Four Madhāhib

The existence of multiple schools is a **manifestation of the mercy and vastness of Islam**, not division. All Madhāhib:

- Are rooted in **Qur'an and Sunnah**.
- Are respected and valid.
- Differ in application, not in fundamentals.
- Encourage **respect for scholarly diversity**.

The Prophet ﷺ did not restrict ijtihad to a single method. Hence, the variety of methods was inevitable and even desirable, allowing Islamic law to adapt across different times, places, and cultures while staying within the prophetic framework.

4.9 Why Should a Muslim Follow a Madhhab?

- A **layperson cannot derive rulings directly from the Qur'an and Hadith** due to their complexity.
- Madhāhib offer a **scholarly path** to safely follow Shari'ah without falling into personal error or misinterpretation.
- Just like we follow specialists in medicine or law, we follow expert jurists in religious matters.

Imam al-Nawawi said:

> *"The layperson must follow a qualified scholar (Mufti) in religious rulings, just as a patient follows a doctor in medical treatment."*

4.10 Unity of Aqeedah – The Foundation of All Madhāhib

It is essential for every Muslim to understand that **the Aqeedah (core beliefs) of all four Imams and their respective schools are the same.** The foundation of faith in Islam—belief in **Tawhid (Oneness of Allah),**

Prophethood of Muhammad ﷺ, Angels, Books, Divine Decree, Day of

Judgment and all essentials of the Islamic creed—are uniformly held by all Imams and their followers.

Imam Abu Hanifah, Imam Malik, Imam Shafi'i, and Imam Ahmad ibn Hanbal—may Allah be pleased with them all—shared **the same creed and theology**. Their love for the Prophet Muhammad ﷺ, reverence for the Companions, belief in the unseen, and submission to divine decree were all firmly established and unwavering. They never deviated in matters of **Iman (faith)**, **Aqeedah (creed)**, or **Usul (foundations of religion)**.

The **differences only arose in the application of legal rulings (Fiqh)**—matters like the method of prayer, purification, or inheritance—based on different understandings of Hadith, principles of legal deduction, and local contexts. These **divergences are scholarly, not theological**, and are a sign of the richness of Islamic scholarship, not division.

4.11 Following a Madhhab: Implementation With Correct Aqeedah

It is vital to recognize that **following a Madhhab means adopting both its methodology in legal practice (Fiqh) and remaining steadfast upon the true Islamic Aqeedah** that the great Imams upheld.

A person who **only follows the outward rulings (practical implementation)** but **compromises or alters the core beliefs of Islam** deviates from the path of righteousness. The form of worship is not sufficient without correct belief, just as belief is not complete without correct practice. **Both Aqeedah and Implementation are essential components of the Deen (Religion)**.

As our scholars have stated:

> *"The straight path consists of sound beliefs (Aqeedah), correct practices (Fiqh), noble character (Akhlaq), and spiritual refinement (Tazkiyah). All these dimensions are interdependent."*

One can follow **any one of the four valid Madhāhib**, and still reach the ultimate goal—**the pleasure of Allah and the success in the Hereafter**, as long as the individual remains sincere, committed, and upon the correct Aqeedah. **All four Madhāhib are correct and lead to salvation** when adhered to with sincerity and proper understanding.

However, **those who abandon the creed of the Imams**, distort theology, or introduce foreign ideologies while selectively following legal rulings are **not following the true path of Islam**, even if their outer actions appear correct. Sound Aqeedah is the **foundation of every righteous action**.

4.12 Final Words: Unity, Respect, and Knowledge

We must never allow jurisprudential differences to divide us. Islam encourages **mutual respect and intellectual tolerance** among all schools of thought while holding firmly to the **unified creed of Islam**.

In summary:

- All Madhāhib are valid.
- All Imams had the same Aqeedah.
- Legal differences are scholarly, not theological.
- One must follow both **Aqeedah and Fiqh** sincerely.
- Disregarding Aqeedah leads to misguidance.
- Unity of the Ummah lies in understanding, not rejecting, our rich legal heritage.

> *"This Ummah will never unite upon misguidance."*
> **(Hadith – Ibn Majah, Tirmidhi)**

4.13 Conclusion: A Legacy of Sacred Scholarship

The four Madhāhib represent the intellectual and spiritual legacy of Islam. Each school is deeply rooted in the Qur'an and Sunnah and serves as a structured gateway for the correct application of Shari'ah in our lives. These schools are not sects but pathways of disciplined legal reasoning that maintain the unity of Islam amidst diversity of thought.

They reflect the mercy, flexibility, and depth of our Deen, accommodating the evolving circumstances of Muslim societies throughout history while preserving the prophetic message. in its essence. By adhering to a Madhhab, one ensures that their worship, transactions, and day-to-day practices are in harmony with the guidance of qualified scholarship.

Importantly, this adherence must be coupled with sound Aqeedah—the core foundation that all four Imams and their schools unanimously upheld. Fiqh and Aqeedah are inseparable pillars of a righteous Islamic life. Together, they lead us towards spiritual elevation, divine pleasure, and ultimate salvation.

Thus, honouring the Madhāhib is not just an act of jurisprudential loyalty—it is an affirmation of our commitment to the path of knowledge, unity, and submission to Allah, as passed down through the blessed generations of scholars who inherited the knowledge of the Prophets.

May Allah guide us to remain steadfast upon the straight path, with hearts full of reverence for our scholarly tradition, minds open to understanding, and souls aligned with divine obedience.

"The scholars are the inheritors of the Prophets."
(Hadith – Abu Dawud, Tirmidhi)

Chapter 5:

The Recitation of the Holy Qur'an – Importance of Learning Arabic and Understanding Its Meaning

5.1 Introduction

The **Holy Qur'an** is the **eternal and divine speech of Allah**, revealed to Prophet Muhammad ﷺ over a span of 23 years. It is the **ultimate source of guidance**, a **light for hearts**, a **healer for souls**, and a **code of life** for humanity. The recitation and understanding of the Qur'an form one of the most vital acts of devotion in Islam.

Every Muslim is commanded not just to **recite the Qur'an** but to **reflect upon its meanings, internalize its message**, and **implement its teachings**. The Qur'an itself calls upon believers:

> "Do they not ponder upon the Qur'an, or are there locks upon their hearts?" (Surah Muhammad, 47:24)

Reciting the Qur'an beautifully is a noble deed, but merely repeating words without understanding their divine wisdom is not enough. The soul of the Qur'an lies in **reflection (Tadabbur)**, **implementation ('Amal)**, and **connection (Ta'alluq)** with its message.

5.2 The Virtue of Reciting the Qur'an

The Prophet ﷺ emphasized the spiritual reward of reciting the Qur'an. He said:

> "Whoever recites a single letter from the Book of Allah will have one reward, and that reward will be multiplied tenfold."
> (Sunan al-Tirmidhi)

He ﷺ also said:

> "The best among you are those who learn the Qur'an and teach it."
> (Sahih al-Bukhari)

These ahadith highlight the immense spiritual blessings attached to recitation — even for those who cannot understand the meaning. Yet, **recitation is a doorway**, not the destination. The destination is **deep comprehension and spiritual transformation**.

5.3 The Qur'an: A Book for Guidance, Not Mere Recitation

Allah clearly states in the Qur'an:

> "This is a Book which We have sent down to you, full of blessings, that they may reflect upon its verses and that those of understanding may take heed."
> (Surah Sad, 38:29)

Thus, **Tadabbur (deep reflection)** is the primary purpose of revelation. Merely reciting without understanding, while praiseworthy, does not fulfil the higher objective of the Qur'an.

5.4 Arabic: The Language of the Qur'an

The Qur'an was revealed in **Classical Arabic**, chosen by Allah for its **linguistic precision, beauty, and depth of expression**. Allah says:

> "Indeed, We have sent it down as an Arabic Qur'an so that you may understand."
> (Surah Yusuf, 12:2)

Understanding Arabic enables one to grasp:

- The **subtleties of divine language**
- The **layers of meaning** in each verse
- The **miraculous structure and eloquence** of the Qur'an

5.5 Importance of Learning Arabic for Every Muslim

Learning Arabic is not obligatory for every individual (Fard 'Ayn), but it is **highly recommended and encouraged**, especially for those who wish to:

- Improve their connection with Allah's Book
- Understand Islamic sciences
- Participate deeply in Salah and Dhikr
- Attain a higher spiritual presence (Khushu')

It has been observed throughout Islamic history that **great scholars and pious individuals prioritized learning Arabic**, even if it was not their native language, to enhance their Deen.

Imam al-Shafi'i said:

> *"Every Muslim is obligated to learn as much Arabic as is necessary to perform their religious obligations correctly."*

5.6 Caution: The Danger of Self-Interpretation without Authentic Guidance

While it is highly encouraged for every Muslim to reflect upon the Qur'an and understand its teachings, it is **imperative to emphasize** that **one must never attempt to study and interpret the Qur'an independently without the guidance of qualified scholars** and classical Tafsir.

The Qur'an is a **divinely revealed, multidimensional text**, and its meanings are interwoven with the **Arabic language, context of revelation (Asbab al-Nuzul), jurisprudential principles, and Prophetic explanations (Ahadith)**. Attempting to extract meanings without mastery in these areas leads to serious misinterpretations.

> "Whoever interprets the Qur'an according to his own opinion, let him prepare his seat in the Hellfire."
> (Reported in Sunan al-Tirmidhi)

There have been instances in Islamic history where individuals, due to **lack of foundational knowledge, tried to understand the Qur'an in isolation,** resulting in **fabricated meanings, distorted ideologies**, and even the emergence of **deviant sects**. Some of these individuals, despite their initial sincerity, **deviated from the mainstream teachings of Islam** and misled many others by forming new interpretations and practices that were never accepted by the scholarly tradition.

Therefore, **studying the Qur'an under the supervision of authentic scholars who are rooted in classical Islamic knowledge** is not merely recommended — it is **necessary for the preservation of correct beliefs (Aqeedah) and sound practice ('Amal).**

As Imam Malik (رحمة الله) famously said:

> *"This knowledge is religion, so be careful from whom you take your religion."*

5.7 Practical Steps to Develop a Relationship with the Qur'an

Here are some steps every seeker of Allah should follow to build a living relationship with the Qur'an:

1. **Begin Daily Recitation** – Even a few verses, but consistently with sincerity.
2. **Set Time for Tafsir Study** – Learn from reliable classical Tafsir books (e.g., Tafsir al-Jalalayn, Tafsir ibn Kathir).
3. **Start Arabic Learning Gradually** – Use beginner-level courses and enroll in madaris or institutes.
4. **Make Du'a** – Continuously ask Allah to open your heart to His words.
5. **Reflect and Implement** – Make every verse a part of your life. Apply its moral, social, and spiritual guidance.
6. **Memorize with Understanding** – Even short Surahs, when memorized with meaning, become more impactful in your Salah.

5.8 Impact of Qur'an on Personal Transformation

The Qur'an is not merely a book of theology or law — it is a **guide for the soul**, a **healer for the heart**, and a **manual for life**.

> **"O mankind! There has come to you an instruction from your Lord, a healing for what is in the hearts, a guidance and a mercy for the believers."** (Surah Yunus, 10:57)

The one who truly understands and lives by the Qur'an:

- Gains clarity of purpose in life
- Develops deep trust in Allah

- Increases love for the Prophet ﷺ
- Cultivates a purified soul and noble character

5.9 Conclusion

The Qur'an is not just a book to be **recited ritually** but a **living guide to be understood, internalized, and implemented**. Learning Arabic, studying Tafsir, and reflecting upon divine meanings are **pathways to spiritual enlightenment**. Let every believer strive to move from:

- **Recitation** to **Reflection**,
- **Reflection** to **Understanding**,
- **Understanding** to **Transformation**,
- And **Transformation** to **Nearness of Allah**.

This is the true way to **connect with the Word of God** — and ultimately, the **Way to God**.

Chapter 6:

Bay'ah – A Sacred Covenant in Islam

6.1 Introduction to Bay'ah

Bay'ah (pledge of allegiance) is a sacred Islamic tradition that signifies a solemn covenant of loyalty, obedience, and devotion. It is not a mere customary practice but a spiritually rooted contract that has its foundation in the life and teachings of the Prophet Muhammad ﷺ. This pledge was historically taken at the blessed hands of the Prophet ﷺ by his companions, not only for political allegiance but also for spiritual commitment and moral rectitude.

Over time, Bay'ah developed into two distinct dimensions:

- **Bay'ah al-Imarah (Political Allegiance)**
- **Bay'ah al-Tariqah (Spiritual Allegiance)**

While the political aspect diminished with the decline of rightly guided leadership, the spiritual Bay'ah continued through the lineage of the scholars, saints, and pious men of this Ummah, preserving a chain of connection to the Messenger of Allah ﷺ.

6.2 Qur'anic Foundations of Bay'ah

The Qur'an itself acknowledges the sanctity of Bay'ah by emphasizing that pledging allegiance to the Prophet ﷺ is equivalent to pledging allegiance to Allah.

> "Indeed, those who pledge allegiance to you [O Prophet], they are actually pledging allegiance to Allah. Allah's Hand is over their hands. So whoever breaks his pledge only breaks it to the detriment of himself. But whoever fulfils the covenant he has made with Allah, He will grant him a great reward." (Surah Al-Fath 48:10)

This verse not only establishes the spiritual weight of Bayʿah but also elevates its status from a social agreement to a **divine covenant**. Hence, any form of allegiance to the Prophet ﷺ or his rightful successors are fundamentally allegiance to Allah ﷻ.

Another example is the Qur'anic command regarding the pledge from believing women:

> "O Prophet! When believing women come to you and pledge allegiance to you that they will not associate anything with Allah, nor steal, nor commit adultery, nor kill their children, nor utter slander… and that they will not disobey you in what is right—then accept their pledge and ask Allah to forgive them."
> (Surah Al-Mumtahanah 60:12)

This passage highlights the moral and ethical obligations attached to Bayʿah, showing that it encompasses the religious, social, and spiritual aspects of Muslim life.

6.3 Bayʿah in the Life of the Prophet ﷺ

1. Bayʿah al-ʿAqabah (The Pledge of ʿAqabah)

This was one of the earliest and most significant pledges, where individuals from Yathrib (later known as Madinah) pledged loyalty to the

Prophet ﷺ, accepting him as the final messenger and vowing to protect and support him. This event laid the foundation for the establishment of the Islamic state in Madinah.

2. Bay'ah al-Ridwan (The Pledge of Ridwan)

During the Treaty of Hudaybiyyah, the Prophet ﷺ took a pledge from his companions under a tree, signifying unwavering support in the face of adversity.

> **"Certainly, Allah was pleased with the believers when they pledged allegiance to you under the tree."**
> (Surah Al-Fath 48:18)

This Bay'ah was a turning point in Islamic history and was so spiritually significant that it is directly mentioned by Allah ﷻ in the Qur'an.

3. Bay'ah of Obedience and Conduct

Many narrations show that the Prophet ﷺ took Bay'ah from his companions not merely for battle or governance but for moral excellence and adherence to Islamic conduct:

> "We used to give Bay'ah to the Prophet ﷺ on hearing and obedience, in times of difficulty and ease… and that we would not dispute the authority of those placed over us." (Sahih Muslim)

6.4 Evolution of Bay'ah: Political and

Spiritual Dimensions

After the period of the Rightly Guided Caliphs, the fusion of spiritual and political leadership gradually dissipated. Monarchies and empires emerged where rulers held political power, while the **spiritual guidance continued through scholars, saints, and pious elders**.

Thus, Bay'ah evolved into two distinct streams:

A. Bay'ah al-Imarah (Political Allegiance)

This form of Bay'ah was traditionally offered to the head of state or ruler, ensuring loyalty and cooperation for maintaining Islamic governance and public order. It is a **means of political unity** and administrative discipline.

B. Bay'ah al-Tariqah (Spiritual Allegiance)

This is the **spiritual connection between a disciple (murid)** and a **spiritual guide (murshid)**. It is not concerned with political authority but with the **purification of the soul, moral development, and attaining closeness to Allah**. The spiritual guide acts as a bridge, linking the seeker to the Prophetic teachings and guiding them on the path of righteousness.

It i essential that the Murshid (spiritual guide) has a **clear and authentic spiritual chain (Silsilah)** connecting back to the Prophet ﷺ.

6.5 Importance and Purpose of Spiritual Bay'ah

Bay'ah, in a spiritual context, is **not an innovation or sectarian practice** but rather a revival of an established Prophetic tradition. Its purpose is:

- **Self-rectification (Islah al-Nafs)**
- **Spiritual elevation (Tazkiyah)**
- **Submission and obedience to divine commandments**
- **Strengthening attachment with the Prophet ﷺ**

The Prophet ﷺ said:

> "Whoever dies without having a Bayʻah on his neck, dies the death of Jahiliyyah (ignorance)."
> (Sahih Muslim, Hadith 1851)

This Hadith signifies the necessity of leadership and guidance, whether political or spiritual, for every believer.

6.6 Characteristics of a True Spiritual Guide

When choosing to take Bayʻah in the path of spirituality, it is obligatory upon the seeker to choose a guide who:

- Is **firm upon the Shari'ah**
- Has **a sound chain of spiritual lineage**
- Is known for **uprightness, sincerity, and scholarship**
- Does not call people to his own personality, but to Allah and His Messenger ﷺ

A genuine Shaykh does not innovate in religion or mislead his disciples but cultivates **love of Allah, obedience to Sunnah**, and **purification of the soul**.

6.7 Spiritual Bayʻah and the Love of the Prophet ﷺ

Spiritual Bayʻah is deeply linked with **Ishq-e-Rasool ﷺ (Love for the Messenger of Allah)**. A true disciple, under the guidance of a righteous Shaykh, develops:

- **Love for the Prophet ﷺ**
- **A desire to emulate his Sunnah**

- **Connection to the Prophetic heart through spiritual chains**

6.8 Conclusion

Bayʻah is not a formality; it is a path to divine closeness. Whether in the political or spiritual context, it anchors the believer in commitment, loyalty, and sincerity. In today's world of individualism and confusion, spiritual Bayʻah helps a seeker stay connected to the legacy of the Prophet ﷺ through righteous guides who lead with knowledge, love, and humility.

May Allah grant us sincere guidance, enable us to remain attached to the righteous, and protect our hearts from deviation. Ameen.

Chapter 7:

Bid'ah (Innovation) in the Light of Qur'an and Hadith

7.1 Introduction to the Concept of Bid'ah

In Islamic terminology, the word **Bid'ah** (بِدْعَة) refers to **an innovation or a newly introduced matter in religion**. The term originates from the Arabic root word **"bada'a"**, which means **to invent or originate something without precedent**. In a religious context, Bid'ah refers to **introducing beliefs or practices into the religion that have no basis in the Qur'an, the Sunnah, or the consensus of the early generations (Salaf)**.

Understanding Bid'ah is essential because it directly concerns the **preservation of the purity of Islam**. However, this concept has often been **misunderstood or misapplied**, leading to confusion between **harmful innovations and acceptable developments** in religious practice.

7.2 Qur'anic View on Innovation

Although the term "Bid'ah" does not appear explicitly in the Qur'an, its concept is clearly addressed through verses that emphasize adherence to divine revelation and the rejection of introducing self-made religious doctrines.

> "This day I have perfected for you your religion, and completed My favor upon you, and have approved for you Islam as your religion."
> (Surah Al-Ma'idah 5:3)

This verse serves as a foundational principle: the religion of Islam was **perfected and completed** during the lifetime of the Prophet Muhammad ﷺ.

Therefore, any addition or subtraction from the religion after that perfection is potentially an encroachment on the divine framework.

7.3 Hadith on Bid'ah

The Prophet Muhammad ﷺ gave profound warnings against introducing innovations into religion:

> "Whoever introduces into this matter of ours (i.e., Islam) that which is not from it, it will be rejected."
> (Sahih al-Bukhari & Sahih Muslim)

> "Beware of newly invented matters, for every innovation (Bid'ah) is misguidance."
> (Sunan Abu Dawood, Tirmidhi)

Such Hadith highlight the importance of **maintaining the integrity of the religion as practiced by the Prophet ﷺ and his companions** while warning against innovations that change the core essence of Islam.

7.4 Classification of Bid'ah: Good and Bad Innovations

It is critical to understand that **not all innovations are evil or sinful**. The early scholars of Islam, including those from the era of the Tabi'in and Tabi' Tabi'in, clearly **categorized Bid'ah into two types:**

A. Bid'ah Hasanah (Good Innovation)

> These are new practices that **do not contradict the Qur'an or Sunnah**, but rather **support Islamic objectives (Maqasid al-Shari'ah)**. These innovations serve the interests of the Ummah, facilitate religious practice, and uphold the spirit of Islam.

Examples of Bid'ah Hasanah:

- Compilation of the Qur'an into a single book form.
- Establishment of religious schools (madrasahs).
- Introduction of dots and vowel markings in the Arabic script for non-Arabs.
- Use of microphones and digital media to teach Islam.
- Organizing Mawlid (celebration of theProphet's ﷺ birth) in a respectful and spiritual manner.

B. Bid'ah Sayyi'ah (Evil Innovation)

These refer to **deviations that distort the religion**, introduce beliefs or acts that have no Islamic basis, or contradict the core principles of Islam.

Examples of Bid'ah Sayyi'ah:

- Beliefs contrary to Qur'an and Sunnah.
- Worshipping saints instead of Allah.
- Creating new obligatory rituals.
- Practices that imitate non-Islamic religions or introduce shirk (polytheism).

7.5 Statements of Classical Scholars

Many great Imams and scholars clarified this distinction between acceptable and unacceptable innovations.

- **Imam al-Shafi'i** said:

    "Bid'ah is of two types: praiseworthy (hasanah) and blameworthy (sayyi'ah). What conforms to the Sunnah is praiseworthy, and what contradicts it is blameworthy."

- **Imam Nawawi** said:

  "New matters that do not contradict the Qur'an or Sunnah and bring benefit to Muslims are not blameworthy."

These statements show that **Islam is not rigid or stagnant** but rather **dynamic in its principles and evolving in its applications—within the framework of the Shari'ah.**

7.6 Misuse and Mislabeling of Bid'ah

Unfortunately, the label of Bid'ah has been **misused by some groups**, where they **declare beneficial and spiritually enriching practices as Bid'ah Sayyi'ah**, thereby misleading people and creating disunity.

Practices like:

- Sending blessings on the Prophet ﷺ in a group.
- Visiting the graves of saints with respect and duas.
- Organizing religious gatherings (Mehfil-e-Milad, Dhikr Majlis).

These are often wrongly condemned despite **being in line with the Islamic spirit and done with sincere intention (niyyah).**

Such rigidity not only alienates people from the beauty of Islam but also causes division in the Ummah.

7.7 Criteria to Distinguish Between Acceptable and Unacceptable Innovations

To evaluate whether something is a Bid'ah Hasanah or Bid'ah Sayyi'ah, scholars have proposed some **criteria**:

1. **Does it contradict Qur'an or Sunnah?**
2. **Does it alter any act of worship in form or essence?**
3. **Is it aligned with the objectives of Shari'ah (Maqasid al-Shari'ah)?**

4. **Was it done with good intentions and without superstition or Shirk?**

5. **Was it endorsed by scholars and righteous predecessors?**

If a new practice passes these tests, it can be considered acceptable and even commendable.

7.8 Conclusion: Upholding Authenticity with Wisdom

Islam is a religion of balance—**firm in core beliefs and flexible in practical application**. The purpose of highlighting Bid'ah is not to create unnecessary fear or division, but to **preserve the essence of Islamic spirituality and avoid deviation**.

One must approach the subject of Bid'ah with **knowledge, context, scholarly understanding, and sincerity**. Blindly labeling beneficial practices as innovations causes more harm than good. Likewise, introducing true innovations that distort Islam is a spiritual danger that must be avoided.

Let us strive to **preserve the Sunnah, avoid harmful innovations**, and promote the good practices that help the Ummah grow in love, faith, and knowledge.

May Allah guide us to distinguish between truth and falsehood and grant us the ability to follow the Prophet ﷺ with sincerity and understanding.

Ameen.

Chapter 8:

Jannah (Paradise) – The Ultimate Reward for Believers

8.1 Introduction to the Concept of Jannah

Jannah (Paradise) is the most glorious and ultimate reward promised by Allah ﷻ to those who believe, strive in righteousness, uphold His commands, and follow the path of the Prophet Muhammad ﷺ. It is a central tenet in Islamic theology that encourages believers to live a life of devotion, sacrifice, sincerity, and moral excellence in anticipation of the **eternal bliss and nearness to their Lord in the Hereafter.**

Jannah is not merely a physical abode of pleasures; it is a **manifestation of Divine Mercy, Honor, and Love**, a place where believers will experience complete peace, fulfilment, and eternal proximity to Allah ﷻ.

> "Indeed, those who have believed and done righteous deeds – they will have the Gardens of Paradise as a lodging." (Surah Al-Kahf, 18:107)

8.2 Names and Descriptions of Jannah in the Qur'an

In the Qur'an, Paradise is described with multiple names, each reflecting a unique aspect of its grandeur:

- **Jannat al-Firdaus**: The highest level of Paradise.
- **Dar al-Salam**: The Abode of Peace.
- **Dar al-Akhirah**: The Home of the Hereafter.
- **Jannat al-Na'eem**: The Garden of Delight.
- **Dar al-Maqamah**: The Home of Permanence.

- **Dar al-Qarar**: The Home of Settlement.
- **'Illiyyin**: The highest ranks for the righteous.

Each of these names reveals a different spiritual and physical dimension of Jannah, portraying it as a place **free from pain, sorrow, fatigue, and all imperfections of worldly life**.

> **"And Allah invites to the Home of Peace and guides whom He wills to a straight path."** (Surah Yunus, 10:25)

8.3 Physical and Spiritual Pleasures of Jannah

Jannah encompasses **both material and spiritual delights**, which are beyond human comprehension:

A. Physical Pleasures:

- Gardens beneath which rivers flow.
- Palaces built with bricks of gold and silver.
- Silken garments adorned couches, pearls, and jewels.
- Eternal youth, perfect beauty, and good health.
- Fruits, drinks, and foods of exquisite taste, are endlessly available.
- Beautiful companions (Hur al-'Ayn) and righteous families reunited.

> **"Therein will be two springs flowing. In them will be two kinds of every fruit in pairs."**
> (Surah Ar-Rahman, 55:50-52)

B. Spiritual Pleasures:

- Everlasting peace and contentment.
- No fear, grief, jealousy, or hatred.
- Love, joy, and brotherhood among the inhabitants.
- Seeing Allah ﷻ – the ultimate and greatest reward.

> "Some faces that Day will be radiant,
> looking at their Lord."
> (Surah Al-Qiyamah, 75:22-23)

8.4 Levels of Paradise

Jannah consists of **multiple levels (Darajat)**, and each believer will be assigned a level according to their **faith, sincerity, worship, and good deeds**.

> "For all there will be degrees (of reward or punishment) according to what they have done, so that He may fully compensate them for their deeds." (Surah Al-Ahqaf, 46:19)

The highest level is **Jannat al-Firdaus**, directly beneath the Throne of Allah ﷻ. The Prophet ﷺ said:

> "When you ask Allah, ask for Al-Firdaus, for it is the highest part of Paradise, and above it is the Throne of the Most Merciful."
> (Sahih al-Bukhari)

8.5 How to Attain Paradise – The Means and the Path

Islam clearly outlines how one may attain Paradise. The journey requires **belief, sincere practice, and striving against one's ego and sins**.

A. Belief (Iman):

Faith in Allah, His Messengers, His Books, Angels, the Hereafter, and Qadr is the foundation of entry into Paradise.

> "Indeed, those who believed and did righteous deeds – for them are the Gardens of Refuge as hospitality for what they used to do."
> (Surah As-Sajdah, 32:19)

B. Worship and Obedience:

Daily prayers, fasting, zakat, Hajj, remembrance of Allah, recitation of the Qur'an, and following the Sunnah all bring one closer to Jannah.

C. Good Character and Morality:

- Kindness, patience, humility, honesty, modesty, and mercy.
- Forgiving others, controlling anger, avoiding pride and jealousy.

> "Nothing will be heavier on the Scale of Deeds on the Day of Judgment than good character."
> (Sunan Abu Dawood)

D. Serving Humanity:

- Charity, feeding the poor, supporting orphans, helping the weak.
- Upholding justice, removing harm from the path, and spreading peace.

E. Sincere Repentance (Tawbah):

Even if one has sinned, sincere repentance erases sins and opens the gates of Paradise.

> "Except for those who repent, believe and do righteous work. For them Allah will replace their evil deeds with good. And ever is Allah Forgiving and Merciful." (Surah Al-Furqan, 25:70)

8.6 Who Will Enter Paradise First?

The first to enter Paradise will be **the Prophet Muhammad ﷺ**, followed by the **most righteous of his Ummah**. The **poor and humble believers**, due to their patience and gratitude, will enter Paradise before the wealthy.

> "I will be the first to knock at the gate of Paradise." (Sahih Muslim)

The Prophet ﷺ also mentioned that **the doors of Paradise will be opened for his Ummah,** showing the unique mercy and favour granted to those who follow his way.

8.7 Eternity and Perfection of Jannah

Unlike this temporary world, Jannah is **eternal,** and its pleasures are **everlasting**. There is no pain, sorrow, sickness, or death. The hearts of its inhabitants will be pure and united.

> "They will not hear therein any ill speech or commission of sin – only a saying: 'Peace, peace.'"
> (Surah Al-Waqi'ah, 56:25-26)

> "Death will be brought in the form of a ram and slaughtered in Paradise, and it will be announced: O people of Paradise, you shall live forever; no more death."
> (Sahih al-Bukhari & Muslim)

8.8 The Greatest Reward – Seeing Allah ﷻ

The pinnacle of all pleasures in Jannah is **the vision of Allah ﷻ**, which will be granted to the righteous believers. It will be the most joyous and awe-inspiring moment for any soul.

> "For those who do good is the best [reward] and even more."
> (Surah Yunus, 10:26)

According to many commentators, **"even more"** refers to **seeing the Countenance of Allah ﷻ**.

All religions emphasize that righteous deeds lead to Paradise and evil deeds lead to Hell. However, several crucial questions arise:

- Does any human being possess the authority to decide who will enter Paradise or Hell?
- If Paradise and Hell do not belong to any human, does anyone have the right to declare who deserves what?
- Does any religious leader, scholar, or group have the right to declare people as inhabitants of Paradise or Hell?

Islam gives a clear, absolute, and divinely guided answer to these questions.

8.9 Only Allah Has the Authority to Decide Paradise and Hell

Only Allah Almighty possesses the ultimate authority to determine the eternal fate of every soul. The Holy Prophet Muhammad ﷺ was granted knowledge by Allah regarding some matters of the unseen, including Paradise and Hell, but the final decision always lies with Allah alone.

(a) Paradise and Hell Belong to Allah Alone

Allah says:

> "To Allah belongs the dominion of the heavens and the earth; He forgives whom He wills and punishes whom He wills." (Surah Aal-e-Imran, 3:129)

This verse unequivocally clarifies that no human has the authority to declare anyone as a resident of Paradise or Hell.

(b) Every Individual's Accountability Is With Allah

Allah also says:

> "Indeed, to Us is their return. Then indeed, upon Us is their account." (Surah Al-Ghashiyah, 88:25–26)

This highlights that ultimate accountability lies with Allah ﷻ alone, and no individual has the right to assume the role of divine judgment.

8.10 The Authority of the Prophet ﷺ is Under Allah's Will

Even the Prophet ﷺ, the most beloved to Allah, affirmed that final decisions rest solely with the Almighty.

(a) The Prophet ﷺ Acknowledged Allah's Authority in All Decisions

The Prophet ﷺ said:

> "By Allah, even though I am the Messenger of Allah, I do not know what will happen to me or to you." (Sahih Bukhari 6607, 6608)

This illustrates the profound humility of the Prophet ﷺ before Allah's Will and affirms that even he did not hold independent authority to determine anyone's fate.

(b) Good Deeds Alone Are Not a Guarantee for Paradise — Allah's Mercy Is Essential

The Prophet ﷺ said:

> "None of you will enter Paradise solely by his deeds."
>
> His Companions asked: "Not even you, O Messenger of Allah?"

He replied:

> "Not even me, unless Allah bestows His Mercy upon me."
> (Sahih Bukhari 5673, Sahih Muslim 2816)

This Hadith confirms that entry into Paradise is ultimately due to Allah's Mercy, not merely human actions.

8.11 True Identity of Faith After the Prophet's ﷺ Mission

After the Prophet ﷺ was sent with divine guidance, the criteria of belief were made clear.

(a) Belief in the Prophet ﷺ is the Basis of True Faith

Allah says:

> "Whoever obeys the Messenger has indeed obeyed Allah."
> (Surah An-Nisa, 4:80)

(b) Rejection of the Prophet ﷺ is Rejection of Allah's Message

Allah also says:

> "They do not reject you (O Muhammad), but it is the verses of Allah that the wrongdoers reject."
> (Surah Al-An'am, 6:33)

Thus, anyone rejecting the Prophet ﷺ rejects the Divine Message and steps outside the boundaries of true belief.

8.12 Allah is the Most Just (Al-'Adl) and Does Not Commit Injustice

(a) Allah Knows Intentions and Decides with Perfect Justice

Allah says:

> "Indeed, Allah does not wrong anyone, even as much as an atom's weight. But if there is a good deed, He multiplies it and gives from Himself a great reward."
> (Surah An-Nisa, 4:40)

(b) The Day of Judgment Will Be Based on Absolute Justice

Allah says:

> "And We shall set up the scales of justice for the Day of Resurrection, so that no soul will be dealt with unjustly in the least." (Surah Al-Anbiya, 21:47)

Every person will be judged fairly and without bias.

8.13 Knowledge of Paradise and Hell Was Given to the Prophet ﷺ by Allah

Though only Allah has authority, He granted the Prophet ﷺ knowledge of the status of certain individuals.

(a) The Prophet ﷺ Knew the Destiny of His Family

The Prophet ﷺ said:

> "Fatimah is the leader of the women of Paradise, and Hasan and Husayn are the leaders of the youth of Paradise."
> (Tirmidhi 3781, Ibn Majah 118)

This is a sign of the Prophet's ﷺ special access to Divine knowledge regarding some honoured souls.

6. The Greatest Mercy: Guidance, Faith, and Love for the Prophet ﷺ

(a) True Guidance is the Greatest Blessing

Allah says:

> "Whomever Allah guides – he is truly guided. And whomever He leaves astray – for him you will never find any protector or guide."
> (Surah Al-A'raf, 7:178)

(b) Love for the Prophet ﷺ is Essential for Perfect Faith

The Prophet ﷺ said:

> "None of you truly believes until I am more beloved to him than his father, his children, and all mankind."
> (Sahih Bukhari 15, Sahih Muslim 44)

Love for the Prophet ﷺ is not optional—it is the core of faith.

8.14 Intercession (Shafa'ah) — Only by Allah's Permission

Many misunderstand intercession, thinking it independently guarantees Paradise. However, the Qur'an clarifies this concept:

> "Who is it that can intercede with Him except by His permission?"
> (Surah Al-Baqarah, 2:255)

> "And intercession does not avail with Him except for one whom He permits."
> (Surah Saba', 34:23)

Even the intercession of the Prophet ﷺ will occur only by Allah's permission. No creation has independent authority to grant salvation.

Conclusion: Only Allah is the Owner and Decider of Paradise and Hell

- Paradise and Hell belong solely to Allah ﷻ.
- No scholar, saint, or Prophet has the authority to assign individuals to Paradise or Hell.
- Good deeds are necessary, but entry into Paradise is only through Allah's Mercy.
- Faith, divine guidance, and love for the Prophet ﷺ are the highest blessings.
- Intercession is a real concept but only occurs with the permission of Allah.

May Allah ﷻ shower us with His Mercy, grant us true faith, guide us on the straight path, and allow us to enter Paradise by His grace and the intercession of our Beloved Prophet ﷺ.

Ameen.

Chapter 9:

Jihad – The True Concept of Struggle in Islam

Introduction

The term **Jihad** is among the most profound yet misunderstood concepts in Islam. It is often misinterpreted narrowly as warfare, whereas in reality, it encompasses a broad spectrum of spiritual, social, intellectual, and legal struggles. Jihad, in its truest essence, represents every sincere and purposeful effort made in the path of Allah. This chapter will explore the comprehensive meanings, types, and ethical dimensions of Jihad, correcting common misconceptions and explaining its role in individual and societal reform.

9.1 Meaning of Jihad in Islam

Derived from the Arabic root ج-ه-د **(jahada)**, meaning **to strive or exert effort**, **Jihad** in Islam refers to all efforts undertaken to attain the pleasure of Allah and establish justice in society. It includes not only armed conflict but also peaceful, moral, intellectual, and economic struggles.

9.2 Types of Jihad

a. Jihad al-Nafs (Struggle Against the Self)

The greatest Jihad is the battle within—against ego, sin, and temptation. This inner struggle forms the foundation of moral and spiritual purification (Tazkiyah).

b. Jihad bil-'Ilm (Struggle Through Knowledge)

Acquiring, preserving, and disseminating Islamic knowledge is a vital form of Jihad. Scholars and educators serve as defenders of faith through wisdom.

c. Jihad bil-Qalam (Struggle With the Pen)

Writing, journalism, research, and literary activism in support of Islamic values are critical in confronting falsehoods and promoting truth.

d. Jihad bil-Mal (Struggle With Wealth)

Spending in the way of Allah—supporting the poor, Islamic causes, or justice-based campaigns—is a recognized form of Jihad in Islam.

e. Jihad bil-Lisan (Struggle Through Speech)

Speaking out against tyranny, advocating for truth, and calling to righteousness is a powerful form of struggle.

> **"The best form of Jihad is to speak a word of truth before a tyrant ruler."**
> *(Sunan An-Nasa'i 4209)*

f. Jihad al-Qital (Armed Struggle)

This refers to **just warfare** under strict rules and conditions—always for defence, never aggression, and regulated by ethics outlined in the Qur'an and Sunnah.

9.3 Jihad in Islam: Enjoining Good, Forbidding Evil, and Fighting Against Injustice

a. The Command to Enjoin Good and Forbid Evil (Amr bil Ma'ruf wa Nahi anil Munkar)

A core component of Jihad in Islam is the duty to promote righteousness and prevent wrongdoing in society.

> "You are the best nation produced for mankind. You enjoin what is right and forbid what is wrong and believe in Allah." *(Surah Aal-e-Imran 3:110)*

> "Let there be among you a group that invites to all that is good, enjoins what is right, and forbids what is wrong. They are the successful." *(Surah Aal-e-Imran 3:104)*

> "They did not prevent one another from wrongdoing they committed. How wretched was what they were doing!" *(Surah Al-Ma'idah 5:79)*

b. Hadith on Stopping Evil: The Three Levels

The Prophet ﷺ said:

> *"Whoever among you sees an evil, let him change it with his hand. If he cannot, then with his tongue. If he cannot, then with his heart – and that is the weakest of faith." (Sahih Muslim 49)*

- **By Hand (Force):** For those in legitimate authority (government, police, army).
- **By Tongue (Advice):** For individuals without authority.
- **By Heart (Disapproval):** Minimum level of moral resistance.

This structure prevents anarchy and ensures the orderly implementation of justice.

c. Transition from Individual Duty to Institutional Responsibility

Initially, every believer was individually responsible for upholding justice. However, once **governance and law enforcement systems were established**, this responsibility shifted to **institutional structures** (judiciary, police, military). Still, **individual Muslims are tasked with**

holding these institutions accountable, ensuring they uphold Islamic principles and human rights.

9.4 Jihad Against Injustice and Oppression

Jihad is not merely about defending Muslims—it is also about defending **oppressed people regardless of faith**.

> "What is [the matter] with you that you do not fight in the cause of Allah and [for] the oppressed among men, women, and children who say, 'Our Lord, take us out of this city of oppressive people and appoint for us from Yourself a protector and a helper?'" *(Surah An-Nisa 4:75)*

> "Fight in the way of Allah those who fight you, but do not transgress. Indeed, Allah does not like transgressors." *(Surah Al-Baqarah 2:190)*

a. Fighting Against Tyranny and Corruption

> "The best form of Jihad is to speak a word of truth in front of a tyrant ruler." *(Sunan An-Nasa'i 4209)*

b. Upholding Human Rights

> "Whoever kills a non-Muslim under a treaty will not smell the fragrance of Jannah." *(Sahih al-Bukhari 3166)*

This demonstrates that Jihad is directed against **oppressors**, not **innocents**, and Islam promotes the protection of human dignity for all.

9.5 The Role of the Army in Jihad

Jihad with weapons is the **duty of the organized military under state authority**, not individuals. Before Islamic governance was formed, individual Muslims undertook this role. But post-establishment, warfare became a **state responsibility** under disciplined command.

> "The leader is a shield, behind whom you fight and protect yourselves."
> *(Sahih al-Bukhari 2957, Sahih Muslim 1841)*

The army must act ethically and defend justice **whether the oppressed are Muslim or non-Muslim.**

9.6 Individual Responsibility in Holding Institutions Accountable

Even with state institutions, **individuals have essential roles:**

- Ensuring governance aligns with the Qur'an and Sunnah
- Spreading knowledge of justice and Islamic principles
- Peaceful protest against injustice
- Legal activism and public accountability

> "Indeed, Allah commands you to render trusts to whom they are due and when you judge between people to judge with justice. Excellent is that which Allah instructs you. Indeed, Allah is ever Hearing and Seeing."
> *(Surah An-Nisa 4:58)*

9.7 Peaceful Protest is a Right in Islam

Islam permits **peaceful protest and resistance** against institutional corruption and injustice. Violent rebellion is not allowed, but peaceful activism is a means to maintain justice and social harmony.

Conclusion

1. Jihad encompasses a wide range of efforts: spiritual, intellectual, social, and defensive.

2. Enjoining good and forbidding evil is a core form of Jihad, transitioning from individual to institutional responsibility.

3. Jihad is for **justice and human rights**, not violence or coercion.

4. Armed Jihad is the **state's responsibility**, governed by ethics and international law.

5. Individuals must still **monitor, advise, and protest** when institutions deviate from Islamic values.

6. Islam promotes **peaceful reform, knowledge dissemination, and social justice.**

Chapter 10:

The Remembrance of Allah (Dhikr) – The Path to Spiritual Elevation

The Remembrance of Allah (Subhanahu Wa Ta'ala): In the Light of the Qur'an and Hadith

The remembrance (Dhikr) of Allah (SWT) is a great act of worship in Islam, which gives peace to the heart, refreshes the soul, and brings a person closer to Allah. The great virtues of Allah's remembrance have been mentioned in the Qur'an and Hadith.

10.1 The Virtues of Allah's Remembrance in the Holy Qur'an

(1) Peace of Heart through Dhikr

ب اللهذكر ت اللهطئمن القلبو

"Indeed, in the remembrance of Allah do hearts find peace."

(Surah Ar-Ra'd 13:28)

(2) Emphasis on Abundant Remembrance

اي أاهي الذين آنماو ذاكاور الله ذكار يثكار وحبسهو كبقر أولايصـ

"O believers! Remember Allah abundantly. And glorify Him morning and evening."

(Surah Al-Ahzab 33:41-42)

(3) Do Not Be Neglectful

وكذ لان من ايلفاغلن

"And do not be among the heedless." (Surah Al-A'raf 7:205)

(4) Allah's Remembrance is the Key to Success in This World and the Hereafter

واذكروا الله كثيرا لعلكم تفلحون

"And remember Allah abundantly so that you may be successful."

(Surah Al-Anfal 8:45)

10.2 The Virtues of Allah's Remembrance in Hadith

(1) The Best Act of Worship

The Prophet (ﷺ) said:

"Shall I not tell you about the best of your deeds, the purest in the sight of your Lord, the one that raises your ranks the highest, and is better for you than spending gold and silver in charity?"

The companions said: "Indeed, O Messenger of Allah!"

The Prophet (ﷺ) said:

"It is the remembrance of Allah." (Sunan Tirmidhi: 3377)

(2) Glad Tidings of Paradise for the One Who Remembers Allah

The Prophet (ﷺ) said:

"Whoever says: لا إله إلا الله وحده لا شريك له، له الملك وله الحمد وهو على كل شيء قدير a hundred times, it will be equal to freeing ten slaves, a hundred good deeds will be written for him, a hundred sins will be erased, and he will be protected from Satan throughout the day."

(Bukhari: 3293, Muslim: 2691)

(3) The Virtue of a Gathering of Remembrance

The Prophet (ﷺ) said:

"When a group of people gathers to remember Allah, the angels surround them, mercy covers them, tranquility descends upon them, and Allah mentions them among the angels." (Muslim: 2700)

(4) Keep Your Tongue Moist with the Remembrance of Allah

The Prophet (ﷺ) said:

"Keep your tongue always moist with the remembrance of Allah."

(Sunan Tirmidhi: 3375)

10.3 Some Authentic Supplications and Dhikr

1. احبسن الله، اومحلد و لا إمل إالله لا، والله أبكر
2. حـ لالو وقـ لاتو إلابـ لا (Bukhari & Muslim)
3. أفغتسر الله العظيم (For seeking forgiveness from sins)
4. اهللم صل محمد ىلعد وىلع لآ محمد (Sending blessings upon the Prophet ﷺ)

10.4 Silent Dhikr (Secret Remembrance of the Heart - Dhikr Khafi)

This is the remembrance that is done without sound, only through the heart and soul. Sufi scholars consider it the highest form of remembrance.

Evidence from the Qur'an:

الذين يذكنور امايق الله وعقادو ونج ىلعوهبم

"Those who remember Allah while standing, sitting, and lying on their sides."

(Surah Aal-e-Imran 3:191)

Evidence from Hadith:

The Messenger of Allah (ﷺ) said:

"Allah says: I am with My servant when he remembers Me. If he remembers Me privately, I remember him privately. If he remembers Me in a gathering, I remember him in a better gathering." (Sahih Bukhari, Hadith 7405)

10.5 Dhikr Khafi (Breathing Dhikr – Remembrance Through Breath)

This is a special spiritual practice of the Sufi saints and the righteous, which purifies the heart and brings one closer to Allah. It involves the remembrance of Allah with the breath:

- While inhaling: "Allah"
- While exhaling: "Hu"

The Spiritual Effects of Dhikr Through Breath:

- The heart becomes illuminated with Allah's remembrance.
- This Dhikr removes negligence and the impurity of sins from the heart.
- It increases spirituality, cleanses the heart, and brings divine blessings.

The View of Sufi Saints:

Hazrat Khwaja Moinuddin Chishti (رحمة الله) said: "Dhikr Khafi is that which flows within the heart and embeds the name of Allah into every breath so that a person remains engaged in the remembrance of Allah with every breath."

10.6 The Next Level: Bringing "Allah Hu" Dhikr into Thought (Intended Dhikr)

The highest stage of Dhikr Khafi is that a person keeps Allah's remembrance even in their thoughts and intentions.

Method:

1. First, practice "Allah Hu" Dhikr with breathing.
2. Then, bring "Allah Hu" into thoughts and intentions.
3. This stage aligns one's thoughts, actions, and intentions with Allah's pleasure.

Spiritual Benefits:

- Purity of Thoughts
- Spiritual Growth
- Inner Illumination

Teachings of the Sufi Saints:

Hazrat Sheikh Abdul Qadir Jilani (رحمة الله) said: "The final stage of Dhikr is when the tongue is silent, the heart is still, but the soul is continuously engaged in Allah's remembrance."

Conclusion

The remembrance of Allah is the best form of worship, and Dhikr Khafi (Silent Dhikr through breath and thought) is a great way to attain closeness to Allah.

- First, verbal Dhikr is practiced.
- Then, the heart engages in Dhikr.
- Finally, Allah's remembrance is continuously present in thoughts.

At this stage, the heart and soul become completely immersed in the divine light, and a person becomes a true lover of Allah.

May Allah grant us the ability to always remain engaged in His remembrance. Ameen.

As the great Sufi saint Hazrat Ghulam Qadir Naqshbandi (رحمة الله) beautifully said: "Allah Allah itna kaho Allah rahe tum na raho."

"Remember Allah so much that only Allah remains, and you no longer remain."

Chapter 11:

Reciting Darood-e-Pak – A Dhikr That Pleases Both Allah SWT and the Prophet ﷺ

Reciting Darood-e-Pak (sending salutations upon the Prophet ﷺ) is an act of worship that carries immense rewards and significance in both the Qur'an and Hadith. It is not only a command from Allah SWT but also a means of attaining His mercy and the love of Prophet Muhammad ﷺ.

11.1 Qur'anic Evidence: Allah SWT Commands Us to Send Darood

Allah SWT explicitly orders believers to send blessings upon the Prophet ﷺ:

Surah Al-Ahzab (33:56)

> *"Indeed, Allah SWT and His angels send blessings upon the Prophet. O you who have believed, send blessings upon him and greet him with peace."*

This verse proves that reciting Darood is an act that Allah SWT Himself does, along with His angels. When we send Darood, we obey Allah SWT's command and become part of this divine action.

11.2 Darood-e-Pak as Dhikr of Allah SWT and Dhikr of the Prophet ﷺ

- When we recite Darood, we are following Allah SWT's command, which makes it a **Dhikr of Allah SWT**.
- At the same time, we are mentioning the Prophet ﷺ with love and honor, making it **Dhikr of the Prophet** ﷺ.

- This combination of Dhikr makes Darood-e-Pak more rewarding than performing only one form of Dhikr.

Hadith Evidence: Darood is a Means of Allah SWT's Mercy

The Prophet ﷺ said:

> *"Whoever sends blessings upon me once, Allah SWT will send blessings upon him ten times, and erase ten sins from him, and raise him by ten degrees."* (Sunan An-Nasa'i, 1297)

This shows that by reciting Darood, we are not only engaging in Dhikr but also earning Allah SWT's mercy and forgiveness.

11.3 Dhikr of Allah SWT Pleases the Prophet ﷺ

The Prophet Muhammad ﷺ takes great pleasure in the remembrance of Allah SWT and loves when his followers engage in it.

- He ﷺ himself was always in Dhikr of Allah SWT.
- When a believer remembers Allah SWT frequently, it strengthens their faith and attachment to the teachings of the Prophet ﷺ.
- The Prophet ﷺ is pleased with those who obey Allah SWT and engage in Dhikr.

Hadith: The Prophet ﷺ Loves Dhikr of Allah SWT

The Messenger of Allah SWT ﷺ said:

> *"Shall I not inform you of the best of your deeds, which are the purest in the sight of your Lord, which raise you in rank, which are better for you than spending gold and silver, and better than meeting your enemy and striking their necks (in battle)?"*

The Companions replied: "Yes, O Messenger of Allah!"

He said: *"The remembrance of Allah SWT (Dhikrullah)."* (Jami` at-Tirmidhi, 3377)

This proves that engaging in Dhikr of Allah SWT is a beloved act in Islam and pleases the Prophet ﷺ.

11.4 Dhikr of the Prophet ﷺ Pleases Allah SWT

When someone remembers the Prophet ﷺ with love and respect, it pleases Allah SWT.

- Allah SWT loves the Prophet ﷺ more than any creation.
- Loving and remembering the Prophet ﷺ is a sign of faith.
- Reciting Darood-e-Pak is a way to express love, gratitude, and obedience to the Prophet ﷺ, which earns Allah SWT's pleasure.

Hadith: Loving the Prophet ﷺ is a Path to Jannah

The Prophet ﷺ said:

> *"None of you will have faith until he loves me more than his father, his children, and all mankind."* (Sahih al-Bukhari, 15)

Loving and remembering the Prophet ﷺ is a requirement of Iman (faith). When we send Darood, we are showing our love for him, and Allah SWT loves those who love His Messenger ﷺ.

11.5 When We Recite Darood, Both Allah SWT and the Prophet ﷺ Are Pleased

Since **Dhikr of Allah SWT pleases the Prophet** ﷺ and **Dhikr of the Prophet** ﷺ **pleases Allah SWT**, reciting Darood-e-Pak, achieves both at the same time.

11.6 Rewards of Reciting Darood

1. Allah SWT sends ten blessings upon the one who recites Darood once.

2. Sins are erased, and status is raised.

3. Dua is accepted when it begins and ends with Darood.

4. The reciter gains closeness to the Prophet ﷺ on the Day of Judgment.

5. Allah SWT's mercy and forgiveness are showered upon the reciter.

Hadith: Darood Removes Worries and Grants Forgiveness

The Prophet ﷺ said:

> *"Whoever sends blessings upon me abundantly, Allah SWT will remove his worries and forgive his sins."* (Musnad Ahmad, 19795)

11.7 Conclusion

Yes, reciting Darood-e-Pak is one of the most rewarding forms of Dhikr because:

- It is Dhikr of Allah SWT, as we obey His command.

- It is Dhikr of the Prophet ﷺ, as we honour him.

- It pleases both Allah SWT and the Prophet ﷺ.

- It brings countless rewards, including Allah SWT's blessings, forgiveness, and acceptance of Dua.

Therefore, every believer should regularly recite Darood-e-Pak along with other forms of Dhikr to attain the highest rewards in both this life and the Hereafter.

May Allah SWT bless all of us for the sake of Prophet Muhammad ﷺ, accept our good deeds, and convert our sins into good deeds. May we always live on the path of Ishq-e-Rasool ﷺ to attain Allah SWT's mercy, happiness, and, in the Hereafter, be in the blessed gathering of the Prophet ﷺ alongside our beloved elders. Ameen.

Conclusion:

The Way to God – A Journey of Knowledge, Love, and Spiritual Transformation

This book, *Way to God*, has journeyed through the foundational beliefs, sacred traditions, and spiritual practices that illuminate the path of a Muslim toward divine nearness. From the core of Tawhid and Divine Love, to the veneration of the Prophet Muhammad ﷺ, reverence for his blessed family and companions, adherence to the rich jurisprudential heritage, and the deep inner dimensions of remembrance (Dhikr), every chapter has aimed to guide the reader closer to Allah ﷻ — intellectually, emotionally, and spiritually.

The purpose of this work was not merely to present theological doctrines but to revive the essence of Islam as a lived, heartfelt, and transformative experience. True faith is not confined to ritual or rhetoric — it is a vibrant love for Allah and His Messenger ﷺ that purifies the heart enlightens the soul, and shapes a righteous character.

Throughout the chapters, the message has been clear: Islam is not just a religion of commandments but a divine path of love ('Ishq), mercy, submission, and self-purification. The goal is not merely ritual compliance, but spiritual elevation — a state where every breath, every thought, and every action is aligned with the pleasure of Allah ﷻ.

The teachings of the Qur'an and Hadith, as well as the wisdom of our noble scholars and Sufi saints, remind us that true success lies in remembering Allah, emulating the Prophet ﷺ, respecting the rightly guided predecessors, upholding unity amidst diversity, and striving to embody sincerity, humility, and Divine Love.

As the spiritual masters have taught: the destination is not merely Paradise, but the pleasure and nearness of Allah — the Lord of Majesty and Honor. This journey begins with knowledge, blossoms with love, and culminates in divine closeness (Qurb).

May this book serve as a means of guidance for every sincere seeker — to understand their faith more deeply, love their Creator more intensely, and walk the Way to God with clarity, conviction, and devotion.

Final Reflection: A Message from the Saints of Divine Love

As Hazrat Ghulam Qadir Naqshbandi (رحمة الله) beautifully said:

"Allah Allah itna kaho Allah rahe tum na raho." "Remember Allah so much that only Allah remains and you no longer remain."

This profound statement encapsulates the essence of the entire spiritual journey — the annihilation of the ego (fana') and the complete absorption in Divine Love.

May Allah make us among those who live with His remembrance, die in His love, and are resurrected in His closeness. Ameen

www.ingramcontent.com/pod-product-compliance
Lightning Source LLC
Chambersburg PA
CBHW061731070526
44583CB00024B/3092